Table of Contents

COME RIDE A THRILL

If you've ever had an urge to take a ride on a time machine, San Francisco can grant that wish. Thanks to the city's hills, more than a century ago a noisy, rambunctious hill-defying little rattletrap was invented that has been making history ever since: the famed San Francisco cable car.

For the price of a fare this remarkable relic has the power to take you 100 years back, or catch you up in the moment, whichever you prefer.

San Francisco cable cars reign today as the oldest local form of transit and the last surviving cable car system in the world. There's good reason for this. Built to climb the city's spectacular hills, they performed their job then, as now, more reliably than any public vehicle before or since created.

Because they managed their task so well little effort was made to change them. As a result, cable cars shuffle along at the same slow pace they've travelled since 1873. As for physical appearance, they corner the market on charm. They are handmade, wooden, primitive and slow. As such they are considered quaint. They also can be uncomfortable, overcrowded and cold. Nonetheless, the further they step from their own era, the longer grows the line of people waiting to ride them. In the Sixties, cable cars transported a record 10 million passengers per year. By the Eighties, the figure had passed the 20 million mark — this with a fleet of 40 cars, only 26 of which operate at once!

Figures such as these prove one obvious point; cable cars bask in a renaissance of affection. San Francisco flaunts them, and the nation protects them by designating them a National Landmark.

Fine to a point, but what is it like to ride them?

In short, cable cars offer the best buy this side of Coney Island for those seeking roller coaster thrills, breathtaking vistas, stomach-clutching plunges over precipices falling who knows where. It's not speed but hills which provide the thrills — the greatest being San

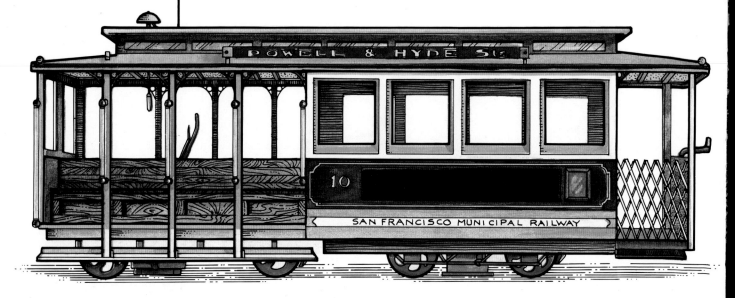

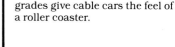

San Francisco's 19 to 21 percent grades give cable cars the feel of a roller coaster.

Francisco's 21 percent Hyde Street hill.

Did anyone say crowds? Around a cable car, always! Most cars offer standing room only, and even that is hard to come by. Seats are a sometime thing, awarded only to those with the wisdom to board at the starting point, or the necessity to ride to the end of the line. Still, despite crowds, one can easily distinguish the native from the newcomer. Native San Franciscans approach cable cars with the casual disregard of any self-respecting sardine; they read newspapers when there's room. Not so the newcomers. They are usually round-eyed with fear, glued to their seat, if they have one, much too busy being terrified to notice other passengers, let alone newspapers.

Hearty gripmen and conductors lend yet another entertaining dimension to the trip. While gripmen (cable car operators) perform physical contortionist feats, depressing or releasing hefty levers, stomp-ing brakes, ordering passengers to stay clear and sounding warning bells, conductors do-si-do down crowded aisles, pleading for fares, announcing landmarks, street stops or jackknife curves, applying rear wheel brakes and signalling grip-men with their own staccato bell when it is safe to proceed. The nine mile an hour pace may seem a veritable standstill to some, but it is sufficient to keep conductors and gripmen chor-using warnings. Of course, few will forget the over-confident conductor who, shouting in his most stern cablese, "Cor-ner, hang onnn!", lost his own grip and fell just as the car lurched around the bend.

Early day gripmen and conductors worked as a team to keep the cars rolling.

clusion the car is travelling its last cable. But death gasps are deceiving, for most cars saw their first cable pre-1900. Having undergone extensive rebuilding, experts predict they'll outlive many newer public vehicles.

The platform crew, as gripmen and conductors are collectively known, is an elite group of individuals, characters really. They are PhD candidates or doctors' husbands or private investigators or former bus drivers. They work the cables for the thrill of it, for the love of people and outdoors, for the ongoing opportunity to entertain and be admired.

Gripmen come in essentially one size: large. They weigh between 180 and 220 pounds, and are long on upper body strength, coordination and excellent reflexes. Nineteen of their 25 days of training are spent on line, operating an empty training car. Only one-third of the candidates pass. Training for conductors is no less rigorous, though confined to only 10 days.

Their jobs are hardly easy. "Some days I get home," one gripman admits, "and everything hurts." Still, when you watch him in action his motion seems smooth, almost effortless. "It's a practiced art," says gripman Max Woods. Some are good at it and they stay. Gripman Sam McDaniels was on the job a record 33 years. Others less responsive to the cable and the crowds soon return to softer jobs.

Throughout the ride the cars create music of their own. Passengers are serenaded by a thumping cacophony of rattles, creaks and groans, leading to the obvious con-

Still, though cable cars remain the oldest, most proficient means of climbing San Francisco's 18 to 21 percent hills, like all forms of transportation they are not accident proof. Runaways are rare but they do happen, with greatest injury befalling those who attempt to abandon the car while in motion. Accordingly, native San Franciscans are warned when young, "If the car gets away, stick with it!" Other mishaps result from automobiles failing to heed cable car warning bells at intersections, or from passengers hanging too far from running boards only to be hit by passing or parked vehicles.

Uniforms were regulation navy blue. In deference to San Francisco's mild climate no overcoats were required.

Just to keep his job, this man worked 12 to 18 hours a day, six days a week.

No wonder he's not smiling.

5

HOW THEY WORK

Rudyard Kipling

In ways cable cars are an enigma. With no visible form of power they climb the city's highest hills and, uncomplaining, carry the transit system's largest loads. How do they do it?

Some riders forego the question and savor only the sweet sensations of the ride. Rudyard Kipling, for one, wrote in 1889, "If it pleases Providence to make a car run up and down a slit in the ground for many miles . . . why shall I seek the reason for the miracle?"

And, yet, to understand the workings of cable cars is to gain a deeper enjoyment of them. And so, with all due regard to Kipling, here follows a singular treatise on how the system works.

The classic single-end car has been travelling the streets of San Francisco since the 1870's.

THE CARS

San Francisco's fleet of 40 cable cars strut out of the past in a blaze of Victorian maroon, white, gold, sand and blue, colors which cars began sporting in 1888. Because the cars are the most visible feature we will begin our exploration of how the system works with them.

When initially conceived cable cars came in two parts: dummy to house the grip, track brakes and a few passengers, and trailer to hold the remaining passengers. Short

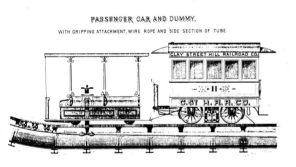

PASSENGER CAR AND DUMMY.
WITH GRIPPING ATTACHMENT, WIRE ROPE AND SIDE SECTION OF TUBE.

years after these cars were introduced, engineer Henry Root decided to simplify. Two cars were merged into one. It was known then as the "combination car". Grip and braking apparatus were in the open front half (formerly the dummy), along with benches for passengers willing to brave the elements. The rear of the car (formerly the trailer) remained enclosed and offered more protective seating. The single-end car was fine to a point, except when it reached the end of the line. Because it ran in only one direction it required a turntable to reverse its direction.

Initially cable car companies lauded the achievement, but in the late 1880's officers of California Street Cable Railroad returned to the drawing board to create their version of a better mousetrap. Designed exclusively for this line, the new car featured grip levers and braking mechanisms on both ends. These double-end cars spared the expense and bother of turntables. When the car reached the end of the line it simply was guided onto a crossover track to begin its return journey.

The same type of cars built to serve San Francisco a century ago are still doing it today. The combination of single-end cars, numbers 1 to 28, ply the Powell lines from the Powell-Market turntable to Bay and Taylor or Hyde and Beach Streets. The double-end cars, numbers 49 to 60, continue to travel along California Street. These cars weigh approximately six tons each, and are a composite of two four-wheeled metal trucks, a handbuilt wooden and metal body, a grip, braking mechanisms, two roofs, two or three bells, a battery-operated lighting system and windshield wipers. These last "modernizations" were added to the cars in the late 1960's.

In Chinatown Cable Car stops are announced in Chinese.

The single end, or "combination car", requires a turntable to reverse direction.

Because they are handmade no two cable cars are exactly alike.

Though they look alike, no two cable cars are the same. Being handmade and wooden, each maintains its own distinctive personality, its own peculiar quirks. To accommodate such avowed individualism, each car is assigned a repair crew composed of men who work on that car from their first day on the job to their last.

Gripmen and conductors acknowledge and respect the cars' personalities, and approach them with not a little superstition. Certain cars are known as hard rollers, or sliders, or good stoppers. Other cars have been involved in fatal accidents. The history and reputation accompanies the car and the platform crew reacts accordingly. When assigned a car they don't like, gripmen have been known to return to the barn within the hour to request a change.

In the 1800's, five manufacturers plus cable car companies' own shops designed and built San Francisco's fleet, which at one point numbered 500 cars. Design innovations were introduced regularly, and competition was fierce to create a new flourish here, a new embellishment there. Nowhere is that competitive spirit more readily seen than in the cars' clerestories, the raised center of the roof containing small openable windows. Seen first in San Francisco on horse carriages, clerestories were designed to let light in and to let smoke from kerosene lanterns out. When first added to cable cars the small paned windows of this second roof were simple and straight. Later, to show off one coachbuilder's superior skill, the "Bombay" roof was introduced. This featured curved top windows in front and back and a higher center roof.

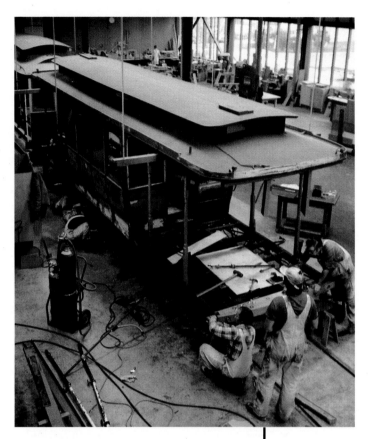

Like cable cars themselves, the companies which manufactured them gradually disappeared from America one by one. Today the only remaining cable car craftsmen work on San Francisco cable cars at the Municipal Railway Cable Car Carpentry Shop. In recent years only four cars, Car #1, Car #18, Car #19 and Car #25, have been built from the wheels up. Most work is confined, instead, to perserving the existing fleet.

The task of rebuilding or sprucing up a century-old cable car is anything but easy. As many as seven trades may be represented, including machinist, carpenter, blacksmith, painter, electrician, glazier and battery repairmen. All machine parts are cast and forged by hand. Wooden fixtures are artfully, carefully reproduced by superior craftsmen. It takes approximately 300 hours to paint a cable car, and before decals were introduced in the 1980's, it cost up to $300 to goldleaf each car.

rebuilding of Car #19, a car involved in a fatal accident in 1967, carpenter Harry Jew from Canton, China, hid a red envelope inscribed with the Chinese characters for "good luck" in a secret place on the car.

The rebuilding of a cable car.

During reconstruction cars usually are endowed with a certain something which distinguishes them, in craftsmen's eyes at least, from any other car. During the

Most forms of transit carry their own engine or power plant, and so are self-propelled. Not so the cable car. In lieu of an engine, power is transmitted to the car by a moving cable dispatched from a fixed, centrally-located power plant. The only connection between moving cable and car is the grip, designed to both grab and release the cable so the car can stop for traffic signals and passengers.

Situated in the front of the single end Powell Street cars, and at both ends on California Street cars, the grip is the hand which clutches the cable. The grip weighs 327 pounds and is operated by a hand lever. When the lever is forward the jaws of the grip are open and the cable is disengaged. When the lever is perpendicular with the street the adjustable jaws open slightly to allow the cable to run through the grip. The further back the hand lever is pulled the stronger hold the grip has on the cable. Capacity loads require the lever to be pulled to its extremity to bear the combined 10 ton weight of car and passengers. The soft metal dies in the crotch of the grip are the only part to touch the cable. They wear quickly and must be replaced every four days.

The grip in use today, commonly referred to as the "bottom grip", was patented in 1877 by engineer William Eppelsheimer, a man instrumental in creating San Francisco's first cable car line. In tribute to Eppelsheimer's capability, it was not until 1970 that mechanic Don Troya managed to improve on the design by adding interchangable parts and a new handle which made the grip easier to pull.

The "bottom grip" in use today was patented in 1877 by engineer William Eppelsheimer.

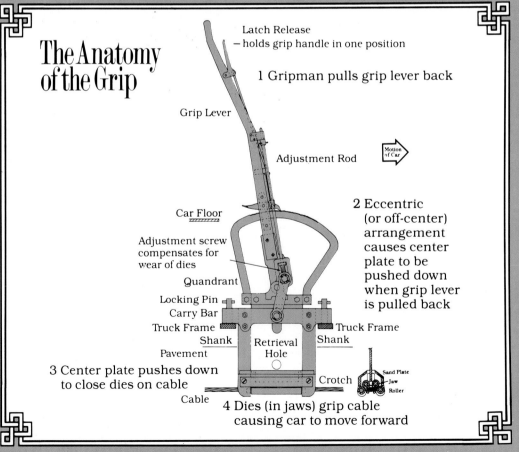

The Anatomy of the Grip

Latch Release
– holds grip handle in one position

1 Gripman pulls grip lever back

Grip Lever

Adjustment Rod

Motion of Car

Car Floor

2 Eccentric (or off-center) arrangement causes center plate to be pushed down when grip lever is pulled back

Adjustment screw compensates for wear of dies

Quandrant

Locking Pin
Carry Bar
Truck Frame
Shank
Pavement

Retrieval Hole

Truck Frame
Shank

3 Center plate pushes down to close dies on cable

Crotch

Sand Plate
Jaw
Roller

Cable

4 Dies (in jaws) grip cable causing car to move forward

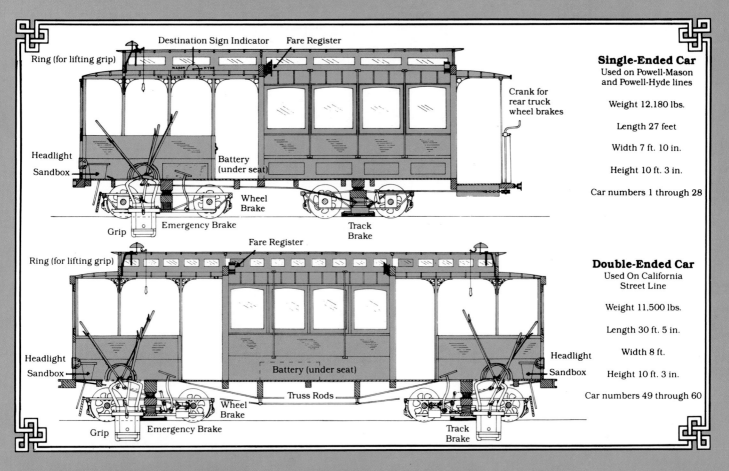

Destination Sign Indicator Fare Register

Ring (for lifting grip)

Single-Ended Car
Used on Powell-Mason
and Powell-Hyde lines

Weight 12,180 lbs.

Length 27 feet

Width 7 ft. 10 in.

Height 10 ft. 3 in.

Car numbers 1 through 28

Crank for
rear truck
wheel brakes

Headlight

Sandbox

Battery
(under seat)

Wheel
Brake

Grip   Emergency Brake   Track
Brake

Fare Register

Ring (for lifting grip)

Double-Ended Car
Used On California
Street Line

Weight 11,500 lbs.

Length 30 ft. 5 in.

Width 8 ft.

Height 10 ft. 3 in.

Car numbers 49 through 60

Headlight

Sandbox

Headlight

Sandbox

Battery (under seat)

Truss Rods

Wheel
Brake

Grip   Emergency Brake   Track
Brake

It should come as a genuine comfort to all who ride them that cable cars are equipped with four separate braking systems. The wheel brakes, consisting of cast iron shoes, are applied to all eight wheels. Front wheel brakes are activated in all cars by the gripman standing on a foot pedal. On Powell cars the conductor applies rear wheel brakes by using a winding crank at the rear of the car.

Track brakes consist of 24-inch long pine blocks situated between the wheels and near the track. There are four to a car. Operated by a hand lever, these blocks bear down directly on the tracks to bring the car to a stop. When applied with particular force, when, say, heading down the Hyde Street hill, the resulting friction wafts the pungent odor of burning pine through the car. These soft wood blocks, manufac-tured at the Carpentry Shop, are replaced every two to four days.

If all else fails, the recently redesigned emergency slot brake has proven almost 100 percent effective in bringing the car to a resolute halt. Operated by a red handled lever, when thrown this three-piece metal blade penetrates the 3/4-inch slot rail. Once in position the pieces spread like fingers to bring the car to an immediate stop. The emergency slot brake is applied only in the rare case of runaways, or when an accident is imminent. These three brake systems are powered only by the gripman's muscles.

The fourth and final brake is the cable itself. By holding tight to the cable the car is checked from going any faster than a steady nine miles an hour.

Four separate braking systems function to slow or stop both the single and double-end cars.

THE CABLE

Invisible though it remains to most riders, the cable is one of the most vital, changeable parts of the system. Like so much of the system, its design has remained constant since cable cars were introduced to San Francisco. Referred to by veterans as "the rope", it is constructed of six strands of 19 wires each. These strands are twisted around a core of sisal rope. Design specifications are exact: crown wires on the outside of each strand must maintain a carbon content of 35 percent or the cable will be too soft and will stretch.

In today's cable car system there are four cables — Powell, Hyde, Mason and California Street — each of which is a closed loop. The cable is routed from the barn to follow the conduit beneath one track. At the end of the line it turns around a large wheel, or sheave, to follow the conduit beneath the adjacent track back to the barn.

Cables have a life of their own — usually disturbingly short. A cable wears in direct proportion to how many cars use it and how full they are. In the 1870's when cars were few, trips relatively infrequent, and loads averaged 18 people, one cable lasted a grand total of 686 days. Today on the Powell Street line the cable is replaced every 75 to 90 days. This two mile cable, which costs $21,252, carries 20 cars between the Powell-Market turntable and Jackson Street, and sees twice the use of any other cable in the system. In comparison, the California Street cable carries only seven cars at most during peak hours. With no turns and fewer peo-

ple riding it, the cable usually lasts at least 200 days.

Cables are constantly in motion . . . in more ways than one. In addition to the steady nine mile an hour speed which they travel, they also experience two types of stretching. During the day the rope will stretch from three to twelve feet from gripping and ungripping of cars and from expansion and contraction due to changes in temperature. The second type of stretch results from age. In its lifetime a cable may stretch between 50 and 100 feet. That's

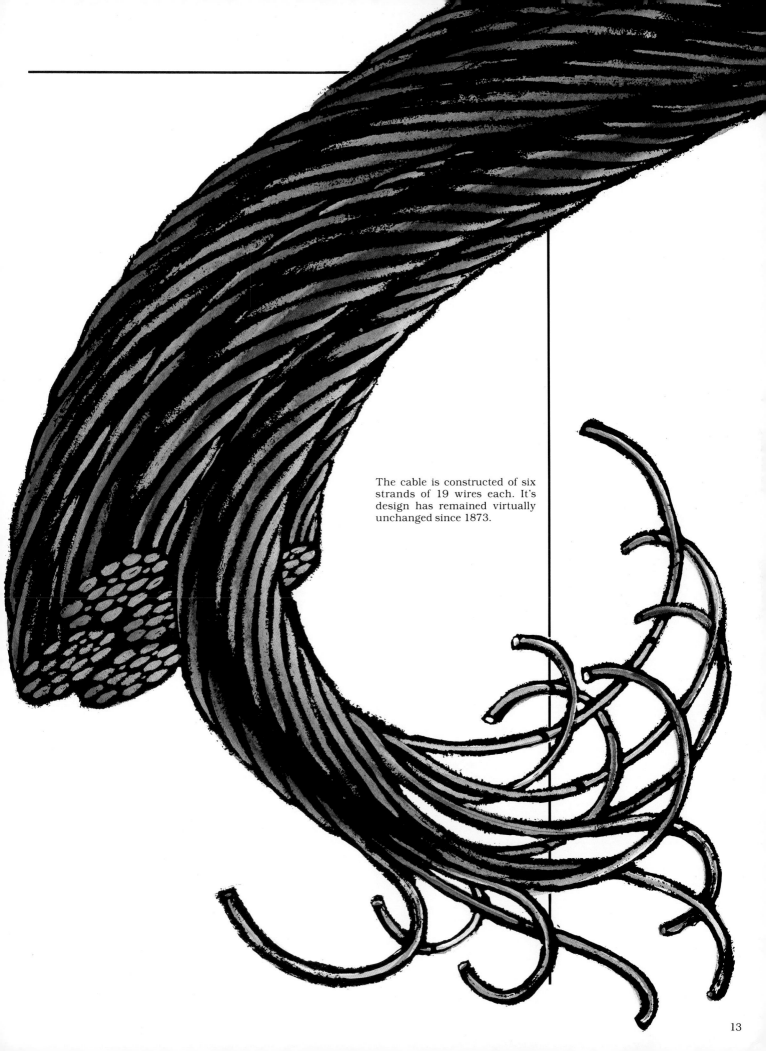

The cable is constructed of six strands of 19 wires each. It's design has remained virtually unchanged since 1873.

13

where the splicer comes in. More formally known as Wire Rope Cable Maintenance Mechanics, splicers inspect cables daily for signs of wear. As a cable approaches the end of its life cycle new cable is ordered and replacement is scheduled.

Cable replacements are staged about 12 times a year in the cable car barn. Performed between 1:00 and 6:00 a.m. when the system is shut down, this demanding job requires the concentration and muscle of 10 skilled splicers. First the new cable on its drum (with a combined weight of 35 tons) is hoisted onto a device called a holdback. The old cable is cut. One end is attached to the new cable via a 30-foot long temporary splice; the other end is

During "the marriage" six opposing strands of cable are merged.

fed onto an empty drum on a motorized winch. The new cable is then pulled into the slot behind the old by winding machinery which is run at half speed. When the splice returns to the barn the old rope is cut off and sent for scrap.

To forge the cable into one continuous loop splicers perform an intricate operation. First, each end of the cable is unwound and laid back for 51 feet. Next splicers cut and remove the sisal core. Then comes the marriage, a process in which each of the six opposing strands are joined. Each merged strand is then retwisted and beaten into place by mallets. The strands are then wrapped in canvas and the many small bends, caused by the

work to this point, are laboriously straightened out. Once completed, the strands in their canvas wrapping are placed at the core of the cable where the sisal rope once was. The process of positioning a strand at the core is known as taking a tuck. Six tucks are spaced out evenly along the 102-foot splice. The cable is then heavily lubricated with pine tar, and is ready to go.

Cables rarely break all the way through. Instead, individual wires or strands may break from friction from track pulleys and grips. Initially crown wires will crack and break. If undetected a chain reaction may occur. Within minutes the cable may unravel, creating a massive spaghetti-like tangle of dense wires coursing through the trough. It is an accident waiting to happen. In 1971, the Powell Street cable unstranded, producing a five car rear end collision at the Market Street turntable. Damage to cars and terminal facilities was $100,000.

Strand alarms work to prevent such travesty. A total of 60 strand alarms, which resemble enlarged tuning forks, are stationed throughout the track's conduit. When a cable wire breaks its raised surface makes contact with a prong and instantly triggers an alarm in the Washington-Mason carbarn. Within five seconds both winding machinery and cable are stopped. A large computerized console graphically depicts the exact location of the trouble and a street repair crew is dispatched. If necessary, the crew performs a temporary splice and the cable is wound slowly back to the barn. The wire is then clipped and retucked and the temporary splice removed. While repairs are being performed no cars served by that cable move on the street.

The intricate process of splicing requires the muscle and skill of 10 experienced workers.

To produce a cable with a uniform diameter, six tucks are taken in the 102-foot splice.

Once these men complete taking the tuck, the cable is lubricated with pine tar then it is ready to roll.

Picking Up the Cable

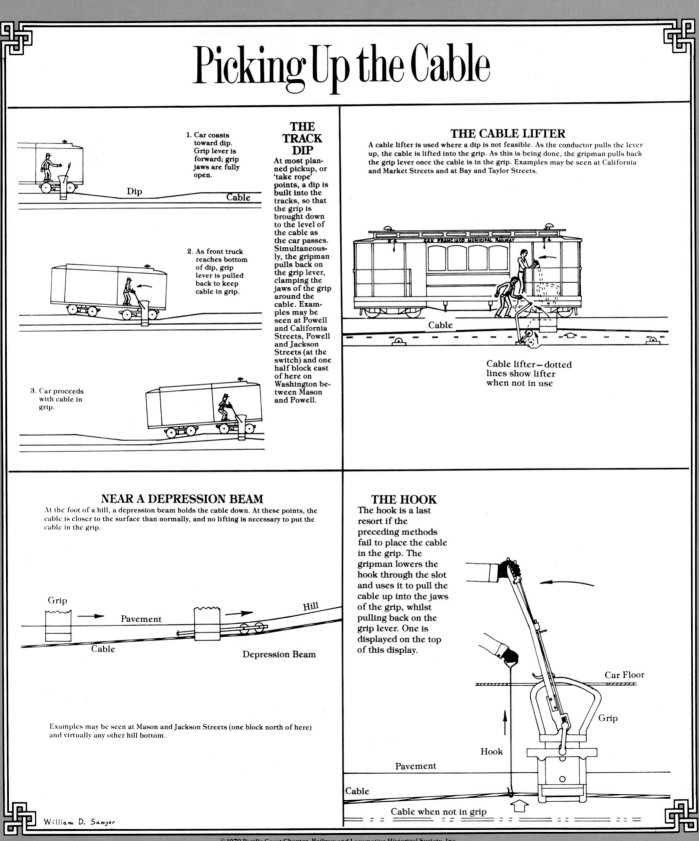

1. Car coasts toward dip. Grip lever is forward; grip jaws are fully open.

Dip

Cable

2. As front truck reaches bottom of dip, grip lever is pulled back to keep cable in grip.

3. Car proceeds with cable in grip.

THE TRACK DIP

At most planned pickup, or 'take rope' points, a dip is built into the tracks, so that the grip is brought down to the level of the cable as the car passes. Simultaneously, the gripman pulls back on the grip lever, clamping the jaws of the grip around the cable. Examples may be seen at Powell and California Streets, Powell and Jackson Streets (at the switch) and one half block east of here on Washington between Mason and Powell.

THE CABLE LIFTER

A cable lifter is used where a dip is not feasible. As the conductor pulls the lever up, the cable is lifted into the grip. As this is being done, the gripman pulls back the grip lever once the cable is in the grip. Examples may be seen at California and Market Streets and at Bay and Taylor Streets.

Cable

Cable lifter—dotted lines show lifter when not in use

NEAR A DEPRESSION BEAM

At the foot of a hill, a depression beam holds the cable down. At these points, the cable is closer to the surface than normally, and no lifting is necessary to put the cable in the grip.

Grip

Pavement

Hill

Cable

Depression Beam

Examples may be seen at Mason and Jackson Streets (one block north of here) and virtually any other hill bottom.

THE HOOK

The hook is a last resort if the preceding methods fail to place the cable in the grip. The gripman lowers the hook through the slot and uses it to pull the cable up into the jaws of the grip, whilst pulling back on the grip lever. One is displayed on the top of this display.

Car Floor

Grip

Hook

Pavement

Cable

Cable when not in grip

William D. Sawyer

TURNTABLES

Being single-ended, Powell Street cars require turntables at each end of the line to reverse direction. After passengers disembark the cable car drops the rope and coasts onto the massive steel and wooden disk. Once the platform crew turns the car it is pushed off the table into a slight depression which places the grip low enough to reach the cable. When passengers finish boarding, the grip takes hold and the car is ready to begin the trip up Powell Street.

Double-end California cars have an easier time of it. They rely on crossover tracks with switchplates to reverse their direction. The car rolls to the end of the line. The cable is dropped. The switchplate is thrown. Car brakes are released and the car coasts onto the return track where the cable is again gripped. And they're ready to go!

A dedicated crew of 28 work to keep the track in running order. Each morning men walk the length of each of the three lines to carefully inspect and note problem areas. Oilers are then dispatched to oil and repair pulleys, while cleanup crews regularly clean the trough of accumulated pine tar, grime, dirt and paper which has sifted through slot rails.

It takes muscle to turn the cars, even with the help of a turntable.

A Geary Street cable car pushed from the turntable at Geary and Market Streets in 1909.

THE TRACK

Among rail transit systems cable car track stands alone in its complex design.

Unfortunately, because there is so much else to see in and around cable cars, hardly anyone ever looks down! As a result, cable car tracks easily rank as the least appreciated aspect of the system. Nonetheless, they are a veritable wonderland of mechanical devices.

In addition to 42-inch gauge support rails which bear the weight of the car, the track features a conduit, or trough, beneath the rails through which the cable passes and in which is housed mechanical devices needed to keep the cable rolling. The conduit is 28-inches deep and is constructed of solid concrete reinforced by a network of U-shaped steel rebar. Approximately 60 percent of the investment in the system lies in this conduit. At the center of

In 1883, tracks were laid for the Market Street Cable Railway. This photo, shot at Market and Haight Streets, shows yokes, switches and pull-curve pulleys.

the track is a slot and slot rails through which the shank of the grip passes to reach the cable.

Contrary to all appearances, the track does not just lie there bearing up under the strain of it all. It and its mechanical appurtenances are working just as hard as any other part of the system. Besides providing a manueverable surface for the cars it also helps keep the cable rolling and within easy reach of the grip. To accomplish this a series of nine inch carrier pulleys are installed every 60 feet throughout the trough. These support the weight of the rope and place it within reach of the grip.

At the top and bottom of hills the track works to prevent the cable from rubbing on the underside of the slot rails. At the bottom of steep hills depression beams are installed. These are elongated steel beams with inset pulleys. The beam, which moves like a swinging arm, is connected to a counterweight on one side. As the car approaches the weight of the grip forces the depression beam aside. Once the grip passes, the beam resumes its original position with the rope once again held down by the pulleys.

At the outset cable car companies shunned curves for the simple reason they had no way of keeping the car on track as it rounded a corner.

That changed in the 1880's when, in New Zealand, one engineer designed the "pull curve", and one San Francisco cable car company introduced the "let go" curve. Both were quickly incorporated into the tracking system. Today, as a result, cable cars maneuver corners in one of two ways: either they let go of the cable and coast around, or they are pulled around.

The safety latch is one device that is heard but not seen. It is situated at the top of every significant hill. Once an upward bound car crests the brow, the safety latch locks behind the grip (with three distinctive clicks) and prevents it, and therefore the car, from slipping back down.

Perhaps the most complex assemblage of track devices are located at the intersection of Powell and California Streets. Here four tracks and four moving cables cross. To prevent constant severing of cables and accidents, certain priorities were established. Being the older of two lines, the California Street cable was granted the superior, or upper, position. Because the Powell cable passes beneath the superior cable, the Powell car must drop its rope as it approaches the intersection, then pick it up again before it proceeds down Powell Street. Certain built-in "encouragements" ensure this procedure is followed.

As the car approaches the cable crossing a "Let Go" point is clearly marked on the pavement. If the gripman fails to respond, the cable turns a wheel which rings a loud bell. If the rope is not dropped immediately, it strikes a bumper bar and is literally torn from the grip. Both grip and cable suffer damage in the process. Once past the bisecting cables a slight depression in the track enables the gripman to regain its hold on the rope before starting his descent.

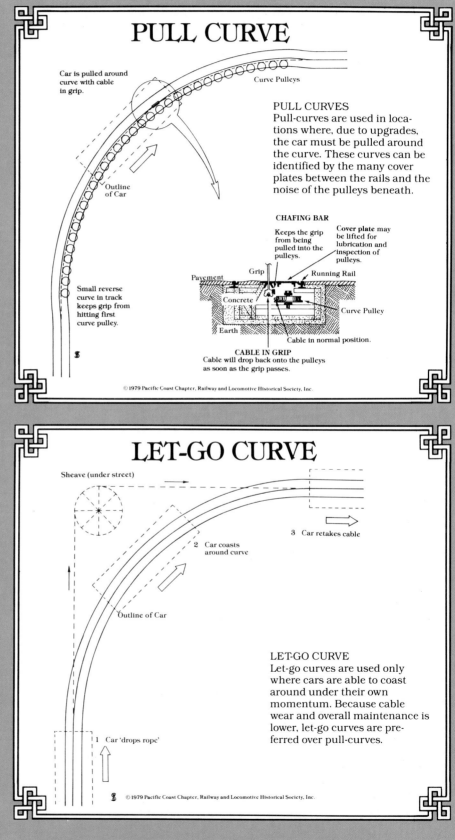

PULL CURVE

Car is pulled around curve with cable in grip.

Curve Pulleys

PULL CURVES
Pull-curves are used in locations where, due to upgrades, the car must be pulled around the curve. These curves can be identified by the many cover plates between the rails and the noise of the pulleys beneath.

Outline of Car

CHAFING BAR
Keeps the grip from being pulled into the pulleys.

Cover plate may be lifted for lubrication and inspection of pulleys.

Small reverse curve in track keeps grip from hitting first curve pulley.

Pavement   Grip   Running Rail
Concrete
Earth   Curve Pulley
Cable in normal position.

CABLE IN GRIP
Cable will drop back onto the pulleys as soon as the grip passes.

LET-GO CURVE

Sheave (under street)

3 Car retakes cable

2 Car coasts around curve

Outline of Car

LET-GO CURVE
Let-go curves are used only where cars are able to coast around under their own momentum. Because cable wear and overall maintenance is lower, let-go curves are preferred over pull-curves.

1 Car 'drops rope'

THE CARBARN

If one were to identify the heart of the system it would be the cable carbarn, located at Washington and Mason Streets. Here cables are powered, kept taut and routed to their respective channels. Here cars are stored at night. Here thousands of visitors flock yearly to view cables in operation and, in the museum, to probe a little deeper into the lore of cable cars.

The mighty roar which ricochets off the walls of the carbarn 19 hours a day emanates from four electric motors and the eight drive and idler sheaves which they turn. These along with four gear reducers constitute the cable winding machinery. They are the power behind the system.

Following underground tunnels, the cable enters the carbarn via a subterranean vault, the sheave room. Here it is routed by 8½ foot diameter sheaves (wheels with

The eight drive and idler sheaves are the wheels around which the cables turn to be powered.

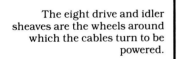

grooved rims), to a trough leading directly to the massive sheaves which drive the cable. Following the course of a figure-8, it travels under, up, over and down one 14-foot sheave, transfers to an adjacent 14-foot sheave to complete the figure, then travels straight back to a third massive sheave, the tension wheel. Once travelling around this it follows the trough back to the sheave room to be rerouted by another 8½ foot sheave to the underground tunnel that leads eventually to the appropriate cable trough.

Each of the four cables are powered by one 510 horsepower electric motor, a gear reducer, a driving sheave and an idler sheave. Because each cable is driven independently, if problems develop with the line, only that one cable need be shut down. It is estimated that the motors utilize only 10 percent of their capacity, though workloads vary depending on the number of cars using the cable at one time. Each motor drives one end of a gear reducer, whose job it is to convert the torque of the motor to the equivalent of nine miles an hour. This in turn is connected to the driving sheave. The cable is powered by the friction it gains as it wraps three-quarters of the way around this sheave. The idler sheave, which is not powered, serves to reverse the direction of the cable and send it back to the tension wheel. The grooves of both sheaves are lined with polyurethane lagging which minimizes cable wear and stretch.

Tension wheels keep the cable taut. Without them cable cars could not operate. By their intricate design, engineered by Henry Root in 1883, they are able to take up both short-term slack caused by gripping and ungripping, and the stretch that occurs with aging of the cable. The tension wheel is mounted on a top carriage which in turn rests on a bottom carriage which is supported on rails built over a trough. The top carriage, held in position by a counterweight, moves back and forth as the stress changes on the cable from gripping and ungripping of the cars. As the cable stretches with age, the bottom carriage (with top in tow) is pulled back on the track using a block and tackle. The tension wheel travels on two 70-foot long rails. When it reaches the end of the rail the cable is cut, shortened 102 feet, and respliced. Before the cable is remounted the tension wheel is repositioned near the start of the 70-foot track to resume its gradual

march to the rear of the barn. By the time it completes its second journey the cable is ready for retirement.

Cable cars spend off-duty hours on the second floor of the barn. Before rolling the car out for the day, mechanics inspect it using a pit under the track. Light repairs and touchups are performed on site. Carpentry is done upstairs, while grips and brake parts are repaired by the metal shop downstairs. If a car requires heavy repair or reconstruction it is transported by flatbed truck to the Cable Car Carpentry Shop.

The highlight of the carbarn for visitors is the cable car museum. Located on the mezzanine, it gives visitors the chance to view cables and winding machinery in action, and with its artful display of memorabilia, to take a tour of the past. Developed by the Railway and Locomotive Historical Society, the museum opened in 1973. A viewing platform permits viewers to observe the workings of the system. Open daily from 10:00 a.m. to 6:00 p.m., it is a must-see for anyone who seeks a better understanding of the past and present of cable cars.

Come dawn, the first cable car leaves the carbarn.

A must for sightseeers —The cable carbarn at Washington and Mason Streets.

HOW IT ALL BEGAN

Within six months of the discovery of gold at Sutter's Mill in 1848, San Francisco's population had swelled from 2,500 to 25,000, and the matter of getting to and fro had become a problem. Streets, what there were of them, were dirt — or mud — depending on the season. The winter of 1849, which saw 50 inches of rain, found mules, miners and respectable citizens wallowing up to their necks in mud, and drunks drowning in it. Barrels, ships' riggings and wooden crates were sacrificed to make roadways passable. Then some clever soul engaged the redwood plank,

Two decades after the omnibus was introduced to the streets of San Francisco, horsedrawn carriages were still the leading form of public transport.

and the first official plank road was born. It followed a 3-1/2 mile path from the Post Office at Clay and Kearny Streets, along Kearny to Mission, ending at Mission Dolores.

Over this rickety biway traveled the city's first public transit, a horse-drawn omnibus known as the Yellow Line. Fare was fifty cents on weekdays, $1 on Sundays. Others were quick to follow suit, and by 1857, four omnibus lines travelled the city's plank roads and competition had forced the fare down to a dime.

Problem-free transportation it was not. Horses, which cost up to $200, wearied after two hours of service, and usually lived no longer than 4-1/2 years. Then, too, there were the horses' daily droppings to contend with, an average of 10 pounds per horse, all of which carried the threat of tetanus and made roads slippery and dangerous to tread. Finall, there was a limit to where horse carriages could go. Hills, for one, were to be avoided at all costs.

In the 1850's in the eastern United States, new components were introduced to local transportation to spare the horses. From railroads came flanged wheels upon iron rails. Metal wheels on metal rails greatly relieved the friction, allowing the horse to pull increased weight with less effort. Next came the steam locomotive which, when coupled with passenger cars, carried more people faster and with greater ease. In 1860, the little steam cars were tried on Market Street. Unfortunately, the noisy, steamy emissions made horses bolt and private carriages and horsecars overturn.

So pervasive was the disaster that the Market Street line engaged one gentleman on horseback to announce the approach of the locomotive by riding ahead of it while waving flags and ringing bells. Public protestation brought about the cars' demise on the streets of San Francisco by 1867.

Because public transportation dictated where people lived, for the first 23 years San Francisco's glorious hills remained pretty much unoccupied. But the city's living patterns were about to be rearranged, thanks to one ambitious, inventive young Scotsman named Andrew Hallidie.

Steam trains appeared in San Francisco as early as 1860. In 1899, this Presidio & Ferries steam train ran along Baker Street to the Harbor View Amusement Resort.

THE INVENTOR

If ever a man was born into the right family at the right time with the ideal set of personal traits to succeed at what he was destined to do, Andrew Smith Hallidie was he. Born in London on March 16, 1836, Andrew had the good fortune to be fathered by a man who one year earlier had been awarded the world's first patent on iron wire rope. From 1836 to 1849, as Andrew developed, his father's interest in and patents on iron rope manufacture just kept growing.

Industrious even as a child, at age 13, Andrew began work as a draftsman in his brother's engineering firm in London. At night he attended school to study engineering. After several years, this grueling schedule took its toll on his health. When his father was invited by John Fremont to test his inventions in his California gold mines, Andrew was invited along in the hopes his health would improve.

Andrew Hallidie arrived in California in 1852 at age 16. After several desultory attempts to strike it rich in the gold fields, he reverted to what he knew best. By age 19, he had designed and built a 200-foot long wire suspension acqueduct across the American River. After that he returned to San Francisco to establish a wire rope manufacturing company. For the next several years Hallidie designed suspension bridges, flumes and wire rope tramways for use in mines in the Mother Lode country. By 1871, he held three patents on a suspension bridge and devices for a cable tramway, and he had begun constructing wire rope from steel which, pound for pound, was stronger than iron rope.

One drizzly winter evening in 1869, Hallidie witnessed a scene which touched his heart and changed San Francisco's future. As he stood conversing with a friend on Stockton Street, he watched five horses attempt to haul a heavily-laden horsecar up the eight percent slope on Jackson between Kearny and Stockton. It was not to be. One horse lost its footing on dew-crusted cobbles and went down, bringing the horse behind down with him. To divert disaster the driver hauled on the brakes but they would not hold, and the carriage began its terrifying journey back down the hill with five screaming, floundering horses in tow.

Horsecars travelled the streets of San Francisco for nearly 60 years. One fateful mishap with a horsecar which Andrew Hallidie witnessed provided the inspiration on which cable cars were born.

Hallidie is credited by some with helping disengage the injured horses. But whatever his involvement, the accident inspired in him earnest comtemplation of ways to avoid such calamity. By 1871, the seed planted that traumatic evening finally broke ground. His scheme involved an underground cable running in a continuous loop to which was attached a dummy and trailer on which passengers could travel. The critical element of the invention was a grip, housed in the dummy car, which could both grip and release the moving cable at will.

While San Franciscans chortled and dubbed it "Hallidie's Folly", the dauntless inventor set about securing a franchise and funds to build the city's first cable railroad. It took two years and his entire life savings to realize the dream. To his $20,000, three friends, one-time San Francisco sheriff Henry Davis, James Moffett, and well-known lithographer Joseph Britton, added $60,000. Local property owners contributed $28,000. Finally, when no other investors were forthcoming, the bank advanced $30,000 against a mortgage on the project.

While Hallidie first eyed California Street, the prospect of generating capital from local property owners led him eventually to adapt his design to Clay Street. Being more densely populated at the time it was the better choice.

The terms of the franchise demanded that construction be completed in only two months. The line was to be operating by August 1. Accordingly, on June 2, 1873, the crews began their laborious task. But no matter how diligently they worked, the deadline was missed. Nonetheless, Hallidie was determined to persevere. By 4:00 a.m. on August 2 the rope was in position and the powerhouse ready. Though

the franchise had expired Hallidie decided to make the run. The boiler was fueled, the pistons of the steam engine began their mighty strokes, and the cable was activated.

The tiny dummy, with primitive handwheel and screw-type grip, four nearly-equal size wheels and leather straps for brakes, was guided to the edge of the slope. Hallidie, two of his partners, six company employees, and Hewitt, an old locomotive engineer hired to take the dummy down, surveyed the fog-dampened rails and the hill which disappeared into the mist. Then they lowered the dummy over the crest only to discover certain inadequacies in the brakes. It was not a scene to inspire nerve or confidence.

Clay Street was chosen by Hallidie as the route for San Francisco's first cable car line.

Andrew Hallidie himself stands proud between dummy and trailer on one of the first successful cable cars. Photographed in 1873.

Hewitt assumed his position at the grip, took one last look over the precipice . . . and resigned his job. Without hesitation, Hallidie stepped to the grip, resolutely turned the handwheel, and away they went!

Fame and fortune hardly accompanied them on this first ride. In fact, only one sleepy Frenchman who stuck his nightcapped head out a window as the car passed witnessed the historic event. But, somehow, his "Vive la France!" and wilted bouquet gaily tossed to the car, combined with a successful trip down and back, were all these courageous men needed.

Later that day the public demonstration was staged. It was not without mishap. When dummy and trailer reached the Kearny Street turntable, enthusiastic volunteers pitched in to turn it. In the process a grip bolt was broken. The delay for repairs precipitated jeers from doubting observers. When finally ready to go, a tumultuous, uninvited

crowd of 60 gleefully leapt aboard to take their first ride. With police unable to dissuade or disembark them, the car set off at a brisk six miles an hour, only, midpoint up the hill, to grind to a complete halt. Suspecting the problem, Hallidie rushed to the powerhouse to find the freshly tarred cable slipping in the grooves of the winding machinery. By adding a little lime and sawdust and placing more pressure on the rope, the car came alive again and shortly thereafter reached the top of the hill.

The experiment was a success. San Francisans knew it and touted it. When Clay Street Hill Railroad officially opened for service September 1, 1873, it took only two days of free rides before cable cars settled into the niche they hold today as a San Francisco tradition. Within months, at a fare of only five cents, they began to turn a profit. Residents living in the area served by the Clay Street line numbered 12,000. Based on a 28 percent ridership,

Hallidie and his partners anticipated daily revenues of $165. They exceeded that goal before the year was out. Within three years, profits were three times what the company had projected.

Profits were being realized in real estate too. By 1885, one reporter described the Clay Street hill as "the best portion of the city for residents", and blithely announced that property values had "trebled since the road was completed." It became a trend: everywhere a cable car line went real estate development followed. Hills that heretofore had been considered inaccessible and worthless now were within everyone's reach — but not everyone's pocketbook. Lots which 30 years earlier had changed hands for the price of one goat now were selling for $10,000 or more.

By 1877, Clay Street Hill Railroad was extended to Van Ness Avenue, making it one mile long. It travelled this same route until 1887, when the line was acquired by the Ferries & Cliff House Railway, which built another line along its right of way.

By his contribution, Andrew S. Hallidie permanently etched his name in the annals of San Francisco history — and in several other places as well. In 1917 an innovative glass front building, designed by the eminent architect, Willis Polk, was erected in his name. In 1970, Hallidie Plaza was named. This busy terminal of Bay Area Rapid Transit (BART) is aptly positioned near the Powell-Market turntable.

He is remembered as a humane man, a visionary, a man with a sense of civic responsibility. He was these things, and he also was lucky. He had the good fortune to conceive of an idea at that exact moment in history when most components were available to him: the steam engine, wire rope, metal rails, conduits and pulleys. He had the experience and determination to assemble these components and to locate gifted designers with the talent to create the finishing touches. (In later years it was learned that much of the design work on the Clay Street line, including the grip, was done by Hallidie's draftsman, a Ger-

The Clay Street Hill Railroad reached its terminus at Clay and Van Ness in 1877.

man immigrant named William Eppelsheimer. Eppelsheimer later emerged from Hallidie's shadow to become a prominent designer of cable railways.) He had predecessors whose experience he could draw from, and whose mistakes he could avoid. In *Cable Car in America*, historian George Hilton claims, "Hallidie was no earlier than third among Americans who attempted a solution via the endless cable." The difference was Hallidie succeeded at what others had only dreamed of or implemented with mixed results.

Of course, beyond his concern for horseflesh, Hallidie did have one incentive others lacked: the sale of wire rope. His company supplied the first cable to the Clay Street Hill Railroad. It lasted two years, three months. The market and demand picked up after that. By the 1880's, Hallidie's company, California Wire Works, was recognized as an industrial force in the city. By the 1890's it occupied one full city block in the North Beach district, and there produced wire rope, wire, nails,

barbed wire and related products.

Humanitarian or sage capitalist? Either way, Hallidie's invention proved so lucrative others were eager to follow in his tracks. By 1894, seven systems operated approximately 500 cars on 103 miles of track.

Hallidie's own California Wire Works produced, among other things, cable for the Clay Street Hill Railroad. By the 1880s it was recognized as an industrial force in the city.

Oregon Branch:
22 Front Street,
PORTLAND, - OR.

Los Angeles Branch:
201 N. Los Angeles St.
LOS ANGELES, CAL.

CALIFORNIA WIRE WORKS
No. 9 Fremont St. San Francisco, Cal.

Mexican Branch:
11 Calle de Gante,
CITY OF MEXICO.

Works:
NORTH BEACH.

The cable car quickly found its role in keeping the growing San Francisco population moving. Here a car stops at the O'Farrell and Powell Streets to take downtown shoppers westward home.

THE FOLLOWERS

SUTTER STREET RAILROAD • 1877

San Francisco's second cable car line, Sutter Street Railroad, started out as a horsecar route. When owner Henry Casebolt saw the potential profit in cable cars he converted the line to cable in 1877 without once stopping service. So successful was this line, following Sutter from Market to Larkin Streets, that in 1878 he introduced the first crosstown line along Larkin Street between Sutter and Hayes. By 1879, Casebolt extended service on Sutter to Central Avenue (now Presidio). In so doing the Sutter line became the first to serve the rapidly growing Western Addition area.

While cable car grips to this point had been operated by hand wheels, the Sutter line became the first to introduce a lever-operated grip.

Sutter Street Railroad — San Francisco's second cable car line.

CALIFORNIA STREET CABLE RAILROAD COMPANY • 1878

Leland Stanford, former Governor of California and co-founder of Central Pacific Railroad, supplied the political might and money to introduce cable cars to California Street. His motivation was self interest, pure and simple. Among the first to construct a palatial mansion atop Nob Hill, he wanted to make it a little easier to come and go. With Stanford supplying nearly all the capital (he was forced to buy 4750 of the 5000 shares of stock), the California line quickly became known as one of the best built, best equipped cable railroads in the city. Commencing service in 1878, the line travelled California Street from Kearny to Fillmore Streets. In 1879, it was extended to Central Avenue (now Presidio).

The nabobs of Nob Hill needed an easier way to reach their hilltop mansions. So Leland Stanford, whose mansion is pictured on the left, introduced the California Street Cable Railroad.

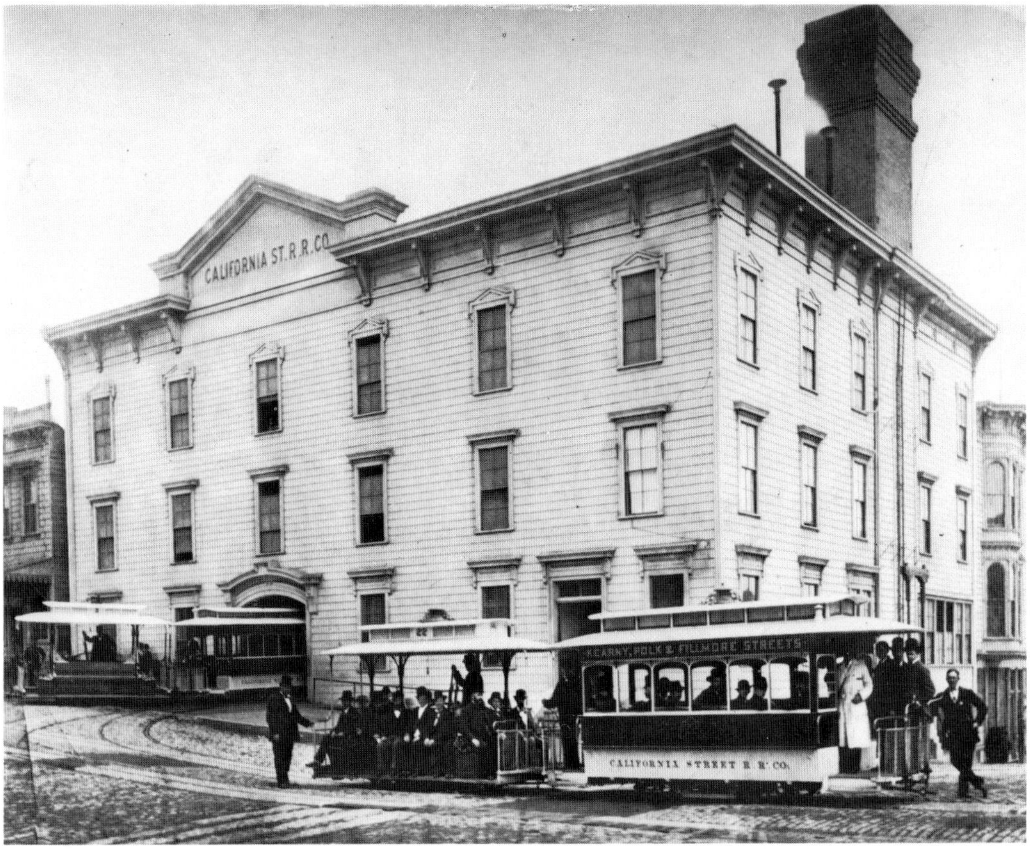

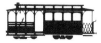

The carbarn for California Street Railroad located at California and Larkin Streets, circa 1890.

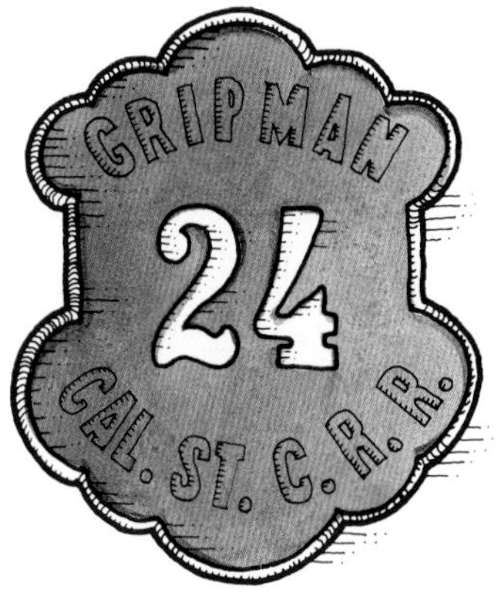

The California line was first to introduce concrete into the track structure. In designing the cable trough, engineer Henry Root reinforced the concrete with U-shaped yokes fashioned from second-hand iron rails. The resulting underground structure was so strong it remained in use between Kearny and Van Ness until 1982!

California Street Cable Railroad was rife with innovation. Its rails, known as girder rails, were the first used in San Francisco, and subsequently became popular with street railways. On its cable winding machinery it introduced the "figure 8" or "American" wind, still in use in San Francisco today. At one point it began experimenting with cable and increased the diameter to four inches. This proved so expensive and wearing to track pulleys and grips that it quickly reverted to the standard 1-1/4 inch cable. Finally, in 1889, it introduced the distinctive double-end cars which continue to serve the line today.

In 1889, California Street Cable Railroad introduced the innovative double end car which still serves the line today.

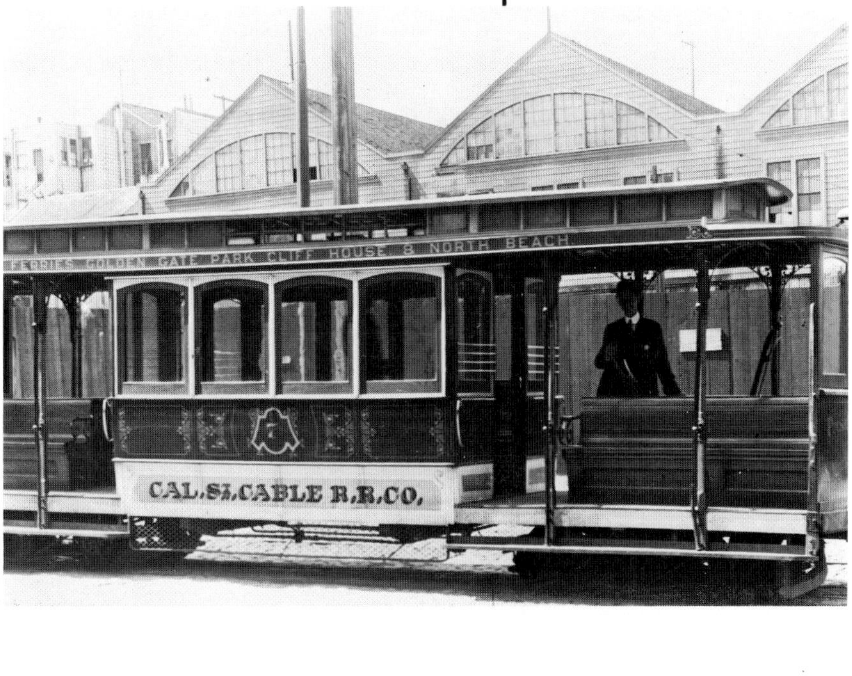

GEARY STREET, PARK AND OCEAN RAILROADS • 1880

Following a 2-1/2 mile route from Market to Central Avenue, the Geary Street railroad commenced service in February, 1880. It was financed by Charles F. Crocker, son of Charles Crocker of Central Pacific fame. The Geary Street line was the first to use the "bottom grip". Designed by William Eppelsheimer, Hallidie's draftsman on the Clay Street line, this type of grip is still in use today.

Presidio and Ferries' cable train at Presidio Reservation in the 1890s.

PRESIDIO AND FERRIES RAILROAD • 1880

The Presidio and Ferries Railroad, which opened in October, 1880, was the first cable line to serve Russian Hill. While prior to this time all cable lines in San Francisco had been built straight, this was the first line to feature a curve. Because downhill slopes led into this curve from both directions, a "let go" curve was installed. With this the gripman would release the rope, coast through the curve, then once through resume his grip on the cable.

MARKET STREET CABLE RAILWAY • 1883

Leland Stanford's interest in cable car lines didn't stop at California Street. Long before selling that line to banker Antoine Borel in 1884, he teamed up with his business crony, Charles Crocker, to acquire a franchise for a cable car line down Market Street. This, the largest and best built system, quickly became known as the epitome of San Francisco cable car lines.

The founders' ties with Central Pacific didn't hurt. Employees were borrowed from the railroad, and many cars were built in the railroad's Sacramento shops. The first of five lines opened in August, 1883. The primary line travelled Market from the Ferry Building to Valencia and on to Mission. Four other lines radiated off this like branches on a tree. The Haight Street, McAllister and Hayes lines travelled from Market to Golden Gate Park. A line which travelled along Castro Street to 26th Street completed the system in 1887.

This ambitious system added new meaning to the concept of rapid transit. It rocketed along at eight miles per hour, and was so heavily used by ferry commuters that during rush hours cars departed from the Ferry Building every 15 seconds.

The Market Street line was innovative too. It was one of the first to incorporate a pull curve into its tracking system. It was the one and only line to manufacture its own cable with machinery installed at its main powerhouse at Market and Valencia. But its ultimate contribution was the introduction of the "combination car", the type now in use on Powell Street. At the height of the Market Street line's popularity, which lasted until 1906, there were 153 of these cars travelling its tracks.

The Ferry Building served as Eastern Terminus of the Market Street Cable Railway. During rush hour, Market Street cars departed from the Ferry Building every 15 seconds.

Ornately trimmed No. 9 car of the Ferries & Cliff House line is shown at the Bay and Taylor Street Terminus in 1889.

FERRIES & CLIFF HOUSE RAILWAY COMPANY • 1888

San Francisco's seventh cable car company, Ferries & Cliff House Railway Company, commenced service in April, 1888. It travelled north and south on Powell and Mason Streets, and east and west on Jackson, Washington, Clay and Sacramento Streets from the Ferry Building to the Western Addition. Here passengers transferred to a train pulled by a small steam locomotive to complete the trip to Golden Gate Park or the Cliff House. In the process of constructing this line, Hallidie's Clay Street line was purchased and subsequently abandoned. But, if it killed San Francisco's first cable line, it also supplied essential components for what are now the city's last cable car lines. Its powerhouse at Washington and Mason Streets, built in 1887, is the same (albeit dramatically remodelled by earthquake and man) powerhouse which activates the system today. And the Powell-Mason line remains the only cable route not to have been changed or eliminated in the past 100 years.

By 1886, when construction began, land prices had soared. As a result, developers built the powerhouse in cramped quarters. To compensate for lack of space, architect Howard C. Holmes (who subsequently helped design San Francisco's Ferry Building) concocted a unique scheme. To obtain sufficient length for the tension wheels he placed cable winding machinery diagonally across the building. It remains that way today.

Because the powerhouse lacked adequate space for car storage, two car houses were built at Central and Sacramento Streets. This proved a boon to the company's future. During the conflagration which followed the 1906 earthquake, all 65 cars stored at the powerhouse were lost. The line's only remaining fleet were those 27 cars stored at the outer carbarns.

OMNIBUS RAILROAD & CABLE COMPANY • 1889

The second largest cable railway in the city, the Omnibus line, was the last to be built — and the first to fail. Blame it on bad planning and timing. Owner Gustav Sutro, brother of Adolph, who built Sutro Baths in San Francisco, and Sutro Tunnel in Virginia City, Nevada, installed 10-1/4 miles of double track from the Ferry Building, along Howard Street to 26th, and up 10th Street past City Hall, to terminate at Post. In addition, he added lines along Oak, Ellis and Broderick. Superbly built though it was, it operated in the shadow of Market Street lines. Too, it opened for service about the time electric streetcars began demonstrating their merit. In 1893, Market Street Railway purchased and began abandoning or converting its lines to electric streetcars. Six short years later, in December, 1899, the last Omnibus cable car ran its course and the throttle of the engine at the 10th and Howard powerhouse was screwed shut.

In the early 1890's San Francisco cable car companies reached their brief zenith. Then began an extended period of consolidation and shrinkage. In 1893, three companies — Market Street Cable, Omnibus and Ferries & Cliff House — were merged into Market Street Railway Company. First the Omnibus Cable lines were killed or converted. Next, in 1902, Market Street Railway pared Ferries & Cliff House's Sacramento line. These two "adjustments" reduced track mileage from 103 miles in 1894 to 79½ miles.

In 1902, a group of eastern investors formed to found United Railroads, a company which subsequently took control of Market Street Railway Company and Sutter Street Railroad. Their primary intent, as immediately became obvious, was to convert Market and Sutter Street lines to electric streetcars.

Of the original eight cable car companies, only four continued to operate as independent agents — California Street Cable, Geary Street, Park & Ocean Railroads and Presidio & Ferries Railroad.

A destination sign from an early cable car.

Omnibus Railroad's Car No. 21 in Golden Gate Park circa 1890.

HOW THEY USED TO WORK

While to the untrained eye cable cars operated in the 1800's pretty much the way they operate today, there were marked differences. The cable, for one, was powered by steam instead of electricity, steam generated by the daily burning of tons of coal. In ten powerhouses throughout the city, sweating men spent entire days ramming heaped shovelfuls of imported coal into red hot boilers. The resulting boiling water produced the steam that activated the pistons of the engine and so moved the cable.

Coal was hardly inexpensive in those days — or so it seemed. In 1873, one ton cost $8.50. Cable car companies consumed an average six tons a day just to keep cables running. Because only inferior grade steam coal was available from local sources, imported coal was in demand. Coal came from Wales as ballast in ships which rounded Cape Horn. And it came from Seattle, British Columbia and Australia.

The steam engines themselves were stationary, low-speed engines of intermediate horsepower. The essential component, given the variance in power from cars gripping and releasing the cable, was that they adapt quickly to a dramatic change in load. The two engines which met this specification best, and so became popular with cable car lines, were the Scott and O'Neill, developed in San Francisco by Union Iron Works, and the Corliss engine. To provide for periodic maintenance and the threat of breakdowns, most powerhouses maintained extra boilers and engines.

The rule of thumb in purchasing an engine was every 1000 feet of cable required four horsepower. Three horsepower was needed for a car of ordinary size, while the winding machinery itself required 60 horsepower. The Sutter Street line happily ignored these guidelines and installed two engines of 500 horsepower each. Only a fraction of this power was used. To run six double track miles of cable with 48 cars consumed only 276HP, of which about 200HP was used to move cable, pulleys and wheels.

To slow engine revolutions to an appropriate speed for winding machinery and cable, cable car companies relied on massive "bull gears" and on rope drives. With the latter, seven to 20 parallel cotton ropes spun around a small grooved wheel on the engine's shaft and then around a 25-foot diameter wheel attached to the shaft of the cable winding wheels.

The cable was wound in two ways: the "figure 8" or "American" wind, as is used today, and the "British" or

In the early 1900's this mighty steam engine powered the cables which coursed the troughs beneath Market Street.

"open loop" wind. With the British wind the cable made several passes in the same direction around two wheels. Originating in England in the 1840's on inclined railways, and

commonly in use in Eastern cities, the British wind seemed the popular choice in San Francisco in early days because the figure 8, with its frequent bending, had greater tendency to break wires.

The cable which originally coursed the conduits varies little from that used today. It was produced by four local manufac-

Broderick & Bascom, who manufactured and supplied cable in the 1880's, is still doing it today.

turers, including Hallidie's California Iron Works and Broderick & Bascom, which supplies San Francisco with its cable even yet. The one notable difference was the method of transporting cable to slot. In the 1800's shipping 40 tons of cable along city streets was no easy feat. It took 56 horses and 10 riders to deliver the 31,000-foot Fulton Street cable in 1895. On a new line, an entire day, 32 horses and countless numbers of men were required to install the rope in its slot for the first time.

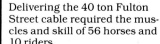

Delivering the 40 ton Fulton Street cable required the muscles and skill of 56 horses and 10 riders.

CABLE CAR HEYDAY

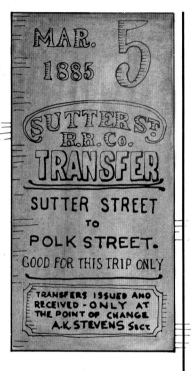

The cable car fast became everybody's darling—with good reason. It had everything going for it. Speed for one. Before cable cars, public transportation travelled no faster than a horse could walk. Now, suddenly, people were barreling along at between six and eight miles an hour! Cable cars went places no public transportation ever had. While horses either flatly refused, or were physically unable to transport passengers up eight percent grades, now cable cars were happily scaling 20 percent peaks and thinking nothing of it.

They were cleaner too. The only emissions, save an occasional tobacco plug spat by an unthinking passenger, came from tons of burning coal. But, in those days who ever considered air quality? Best of all, cable cars cost so little to operate. One year after switching his Sutter Street line from horse to cable car, Henry Casebolt saw operating costs slashed 30 percent. Others who followed found it about 50 percent cheaper to transport people by cable instead of horse.

Truly it was "rapid transit" in its most evolved state.

With seven cable companies serving San Francisco, competition for passengers was fierce. Unlike today, with public transportation managed by government, in that era cable car companies were privately owned. Revenue balanced on quality of service, to be sure, but the more ingenious companies didn't stop there. To put their passengers in a holiday mood, Presidio & Ferries Railroad engaged brass bands on Sundays to play from the start of the line, along Union Street, to the terminus at Harbor View Park. Other lines resorted to what today might be considered false advertising. Destination signs announced places their cars didn't go. If, for example, a Ferries & Cliff House passenger *really* wanted to go to the Cliff House, he or she was forced to transfer to a steam powered train at Central Avenue to complete the trip.

One way company managers kept profits up was to keep paychecks down. The going salary for gripmen and conductors from 1880 to 1907 was $2.50 a day. Shifts lasted between 12 and 18 hours a day, with 20 to 45 minutes off for dinner and supper. Those working for more progressive lines were considered lucky: they worked only six days a week. Others had one day off every two weeks. Hours were as long as employers' expectations were high. Employees were required to stand while on duty. Leaning against a railing or dashboard was a forbidden

Ferries & Cliff House steam train on California Street, April, 1905.

38

Midmorning most weekdays during the 1880's found women shoppers boarding the cars to head downtown for lunch and shopping.

luxury and grounds for reprimand.

Fares, which held at five cents a ride, were always a source of contention. Conductors on Ferries & Cliff House registered each fare on a slip of paper which hung from the front of their jackets. At day's end they were required to make up any discrepency from their own pocket. To keep conductors honest, "spotters" were hired, and they didn't always play fair. One beauteous young lady insisted she already had paid her fare. Not wanting to seem rude the conductor acquiesced, only, the next day, to lose his job for shorting the company.

Trying working conditions didn't prevent crews from playing hero. Newly arrived Chinese immigrants often became the target of thugs. Gripmen, many of them Irish, were offended by the slight and would stop the cars to rally to their defense. They were rewarded for such valor with rice cakes, carved ivory trinkets and rare teas.

Heroes they were, faultless drivers they were not. Of course, it wasn't easy when their paths often were obstructed by drays, horsecars, wagons, buggies, other cable cars and pedestrians. Besides sheer bulk, their only other defense in this free-for-all was their bell. By 1882, the forthright little cable car bell had made its way into law. Simply stated, the statute declared it was illegal for any grip car or dummy to approach a streetcrossing without ringing its bell 25 feet in advance and continuing to ring it until the car had crossed the intersection. It is unclear whether accidents were reduced after that, but groundwork was laid for another tradition: San Francisco's annual Cable Car Bell Ringing Contest.

It took exactly 12 years—from 1873 to 1885—for the pendulum to begin to swing, for interlopers that would eventually replace cable cars to make their presence known. But first came electricity, a silent, clean form of power which wooed and eventually won all former devotees of cable.

Electric streetcars were perfected by 1888, and shortly thereafter were introduced in San Francisco. Because these cars carried their own motors and took power from an overhead wire, they

avoided the expense and complication of the moving cable. What they lacked in charm they made up in convenience, speed, and, ultimately, economy. Besides, an electric car could back up, a cable car could not. An electric car could make up lost time, a cable car could not.

These were the arguments salesmen used to sway cable car and city officials to their side. And they worked. San Francisco's first electric streetcar line, the San Francisco & San Mateo, commenced service in 1891. By 1902, consideration was being given to converting Market and Sutter Streets to electric streetcars. There were objections, to be sure. Existing franchises permitted cable or horsecars only, while many residents protested against unsightly poles and overhead wires.

These arguments proved academic, however, for one April morn-

Electric streetcars attracted their largest crowds in 1912, with the opening of San Francisco Municipal Railway.

ing in 1906, Nature (always the unpredictable one) rearranged the pawns, and in so doing cast one decided vote for electric streetcars.

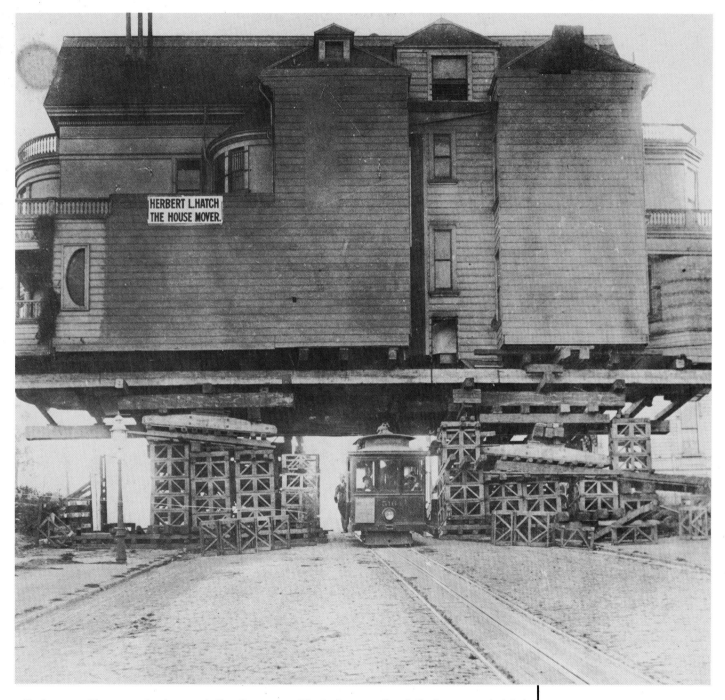

HERBERT L. HATCH
THE HOUSE MOVER.

Early on, cable cars gained a reputation for going places no other form of public transportation could — or would — ever go. It happened again in October, 1913.

One day Herbert L. Hatch decided to move a house. The house was situated on Washington Street, between Franklin and Gough. The street was steep enough as it was, but Herbert had an even bigger problem: how to move a four story house without once impeding the comings and goings of the Ferries & Cliff House cable car.

The jacks were placed, the house was hoisted and moved, and the determined little cable cars just kept rolling.

Whether Herbert engaged in prayers or crossed fingers is not known, but the feat — and the house — was carried off uneventfully. Perhaps the largest loss resulting from this stalwart act of derring-do was a slight decline in ridership.

Who can blame those who chose to get off and walk?

THE EARTHQUAKE

At six seconds past 5:12 a.m. on April 18, 1906, an earthquake struck measuring 8.25 on the Richter scale. For 48 seconds, as the western perimeter of the continent shifted 18 feet north, the town undulated, swelled, cracked and rocked like unsecured cargo on a storm-tossed sea. After a moment of silence a second jolt hit, followed twelve minutes later by the first of a series of aftershocks.

Short hours after the massive jolt the wild dance of flames began.

Heard first in the deadly stillness which followed were the screams of those trapped beneath buckled chimneys, walls and cornices. Early light found the pajama-clad populace sifting through debris in search of the living and the dead. Others hastily dressed and ushered families into parks and open areas free from the threat of falling buildings.

But the worst was yet to come. South of Market Street small fires had ignited and were being fanned by erratic winds. It was learned then that Fire Chief Dennis Sullivan had been killed during the quake. Nevertheless, volunteers rolled out the wagons and prepared to battle the blazes only to learn that in filled and marshy ground, water lines had broken. They used what water was available to them. Then, to halt the

The Ferries & Cliff House cable carbarn, at Washington and Mason Streets, before the devastating quake.

The carbarn on April 18, 1906, short hours after the quake.

The cable carbarn photographed from the same angle days after the fire passed. Only the trees managed to survive.

More than 28,000 buildings were destroyed by fire, among them the Ferries & Cliff House cable carbarn.

wild dance of flames, they reverted to dynamite. "Buildings were blown to atoms," the newspaper reported.

Initially unaware of the threat of fire, stunned San Franciscans spent the day surveying quake damage and searching for displaced families and friends. United Railroads' photographer, Harry Mentz, toured cable car facilities to assess and photograph quake damage.

Meanwhile the fire was gaining strength. Nothing helped stave the flames which raged now at temperatures up to 2700 degrees Fahrenheit. In three days it marched its resolute path across 4.11 square miles, from Market Street up over Nob and Russian Hills to its final terminus at

As the fire advanced, 300,000 homeless refugees made their way to the unburned western part of the city, including Golden Gate Park, to seek shelter. Within days thousands of one and two-room canvas shelters were erected. Later, abandoned and damaged cable cars were converted to temporary dwellings. Because all indoor cooking was prohibited, throughout the city impromptu street kitchens were set up and breadlines began to form. Martial law was instituted and enforced by mounted militia. In the first day three thieves met their deaths by rifle bullets while at work in the ruins.

By June, 1906, the Board of Health had assessed human casualties at 503, (a figure since revised to 2010 by the San Francisco Archives). Property damage was estimated at $350,000,000. Included in this figure were losses suffered by cable car companies. In some areas cable car tracks and conduits lay twisted and uprooted in the streets. Inside powerhouses, steam

engines were loosened from their foundations and connections between boilers and engines were severed. All that was left of carbarns gutted by fire were tangled masses of pipe and ironwork, tumbled brick and mortar walls and the charred remains of car-trucks which only yesterday had supported a proud, colorful fleet.

Hardest hit were the cable car companies whose carbarns were situated in the fire zone. Fire levelled the Ferries & Cliff House's Washington-Mason carbarn, taking with it 65 cars. Only 27 cars were salvaged, and those because they were stored at two outer carbarns.

Fire destroyed the California-Hyde carbarn and all 52 double end cars of the California Street Cable Railroad Company. In the powerhouse, three of four boilers were destroyed, but the triple expansion steam engine and four sets of winding machinery were repairable. California Cable settled on a return of only half its losses from its insurance company, Fireman's Fund.

Then, like the phoenix rising from the ashes, it began again. J. Hammond & Company and Holman Car Company salvaged metal parts from burned cars to rebuild replacement cars. In August, 1906, the cadence of the engine sent a cloud of white steam through the partly rebuilt barn as a few new cars with old wheels transported people among the ruins that lined California Street. The Jones-Hyde line didn't resume service until July, 1908. It took until 1915 for a full complement of 48 cars to be completed and returned to service.

The 1906 calamity proved fatal to the Sutter Street and Presidio & Ferries lines. Both systems saw their powerhouses gutted by fire. Due to heavy damage to carbarns and fleet, both were forced to discontinue service as a cable line. Both were subsequently restored as streetcar lines.

The one exception was precipitated by influential homeowners who banded together to demand that cable service be restored along Pacific Avenue. The web of overhead electric wires required to run trolleys, it seems, offended their collective sensitivities. With just the right political pull they maneuvered the Sutter Street system (which was owned and operated now by United Railroads) into building a carbarn at Pacific near Polk. Service, utilizing a single cable and five dummy and trailer cars, was reinstituted along Pacific Avenue in 1908.

The day before Ferries & Cliff House service resumed in January, 1907. The steam engine is activated, as are the winders, but cars must be stored in the street until the building is completed.

California and Hyde Streets, August, 1906. Trucks from burned cable cars in the foreground.

Because its powerhouse was situated outside the fire zone, the Geary Street line experienced the least damage. On June 22, 1906, it became the first cable car line to resume service.

One catastrophic blow to cable cars was inflicted not by Nature but by man. The Market Street lines, then a part of United Railroads, suffered only moderate damage compared to others. The main powerhouse partially burned and its roof collapsed, while smokestacks were damaged at two other power-houses. Still, fleet and tracks survived in good condition. But, United Railroad executives, in league with trolley salesmen, viewed the earth-

The 300,000 homeless San Franciscans made the best of the situation by converting badly damaged cable cars to temporary shelters.

quake as a perfect opportunity to substitute old for new. In their zeal for change they stooped to corruption. They claimed the cable lines required complete reconstruction. They bribed the Board of Supervisors $200,000 to revise the Market Street franchise to allow the use of electric streetcars with overhead wires.

The bribe accepted, they wasted no time implementing the plan. In two weeks the crew had reactivated the generating plant on Bryant Street, revised trackwork and strung overhead wires. Carbarns on McAllister, Haight and Valencia were revamped to house electric cars. On May 3, 1906, a mere 16 days after the quake, Mayor Eugene E. Schmitz, the Board of Supervisors and United Railroad president Patrick Calhoun rode the first electric trolley down Market Street. Politicians smiled and shook hands; news reporters and photographers recorded the event. But the smiles were short-lived. Within months, Mayor Schmitz was arrested on 27 counts of bribery and graft, while his mentor, the notorious Abe Ruef, was indicated on 129 counts of civic graft. During his trial Ruef implicated four United Railroad officials because of the manner in which the overhead trolley franchise was procured. Ruef eventually was convicted of bribery and served a four year, seven month sentence in San Quentin.

The 1907, Castro Street cable cars once again began scaling the 18 percent grades — the only form of transportation capable of doing so.

Unfortunately, the damage was already done. Cables had been killed, and on all but the steepest inclines, cable cars had been replaced by trolleys. Never again was the distinctive rattle and hum of the cable heard in the Market Street slot or any of its four tributaries. Indeed, the only surviving trace of the once-dominant line travelled Castro between 18th and 26th Streets. Here, starting in 1907, cable cars again coursed the 18 percent grade with historic ease, proving as they did that progress was okay to a point, but not when it came to hills.

The economy and speed of trolleys charmed railway officials and riders alike. On Sutter Street, cable track was removed and streetcar track installed. The Presidio & Ferries complex web of lines was converted to streetcar use. The Geary Street line, which had been acquired by the city, ceased cable service in 1912. This, the city's first publicly owned transportation line, converted to electric trolley by year end.

By the time Nature, politics and progress had their way, the pre-earthquake track mileage of 79½ miles had been reduced to 25. And even these, as time was to prove, were not secure. With the exception of Pacific Avenue, the cable mileage retained was all on streets too steep for the new streetcars to climb.

Life was relatively peaceful for the cable cars the next 35 years. United Railroads went into reorganization in 1919 and emerged in 1921 as the Market Street Railway Company. Besides streetcars, the company operated five of the seven remaining cable car lines, including Powell-Mason, Powell-Jackson, Sacramento-Clay, the eight block run on Castro Street, and the short run along Pacific Avenue. Unfortunately, financial analysis in 1927 showed only the two Powell lines to be profitable. As a result the Pacific Avenue cable ran its last in November, 1929. Meanwhile, diesel buses began demonstrating their might on hills once managed only by cable cars. Being cheaper to operate,they replaced cable cars on Castro Street in April, 1941, and on Sacramento and Clay Streets in February, 1942.

Next, Market Street Railway officials began considering electric trolley buses to replace cable cars along the Powell Street lines. The only thing that preserved the remaining 27 cars at that point was the lack of adequate funds.

Meanwhile, California Street Cable Railroad, under the able leadership of James W. Harris, maintained a constant record of service along California Street, and on its crosstown Jones-Hyde route. Mr. Harris joined the company in 1879. Starting as a carpenter he advanced himself eventually to shop foreman, superintendent, vice president and, finally, president. Mr. Harris gave over 60 years of service to California Cable before his retirement.

The rest of the Market Street Railroad was converted to electric streetcars.

47

ON SAVING THE CABLE CAR

This peaceful interim ended abruptly at the close of World War II. Because of the shortage of maintenance crews and money during the war, tracks, cables and cars had fallen into disrepair. Mayor Roger Lapham, a former businessman who had gained office on a platform of economy and reform, announced a clean sweep in his annual message of January, 1947. Cable cars were out, he said, diesel buses had been ordered and would start service in 30 days.

On the surface San Francisco responded nostalgically, almost passively. Headlines declared, "Cable Cars on Their Last Leg" and "We'll Miss Them". But somewhere deep a nerve had been struck. Something so intrinsically dear to the heart of San Francisco would not be sacrificed without a fight. First to sound the battle cry was socialite and civic leader, Mrs. Hans Klussman. Forging an unlikely alliance between San Francisco Federation of the Arts, of which she was a prominent member, and the California Spring Blossom and Wildflower Assocation, by March, 1947, Friedel Klussman announced formation of a "Citizens Committee to Save the Cable Cars." Hundreds of public spirited citizens joined to badger politicians and gather signatures to place an initiative on the ballot. Their fervor attracted national press. Within months cable cars rode into the limelight on pages of LIFE, TIME and other national magazines. Meanwhile, Gumps, a purveyor of fine art and imports, ran a small insert in TIME Magazine inviting response to the proposed ousting of the cable cars. Within weeks thousands of letters flowed in from throughout the United States and Canada. All but one — a lady whose sleep had been disturbed by cable cars her one night in San Francisco — were unanimously in favor of preserving the cars.

The grim-faced Mayor looked upon this groundswell as sheer frivolity. He responded by engaging a horsecar to ride the length of Market Street. His sentiments were expressed in an accompanying release. To him cable cars were "an outmoded, broken down form of transportation . . . The horsecar had to go. Now cable cars have to go." The gimmick backfired. Charmed by the quaintness of the horsecar, not a few observers felt San Francisco would be well served by restoring them to service too.

The November ballot initiative to save cable cars gained an over whelming 77 percent in favor. It was subsequently written into City Char-

In the 1950's cable cars went against traffic on Pine Street for two blocks. The large sign over the street lit up when the cable car approached.

ter that the two Powell cable lines, then operated by the Municipal Railway, would continue to operate. In ways it was a false victory, for though the cars' existence had been guaranteed, their routes had not. And so the battle continued, in four separate clashes over the next seven years.

Two of these clashes involved the California Street line. After 73 years of private ownership, in 1951, California Street Cable Railway fell to the multiple pressures of labor problems, financial difficulties and a lawsuit which caused the line's liability coverage to be cancelled. San Francisco Municipal Railway purchased the company for $138,000, and soon after began paring its lines. The Jones Street shuttle rode its last in February, 1954, and in May the O'Farrell-Hyde line and the outer portion of California Street to Presidio Avenue were terminated. But not without a struggle. Letter writers complained, crowds protested, sign painters railed. "What sort of city government is this?" one sign queried, "To work so hard against the wishes of the people!"

In 1954, the same city government went back to the electorate with Proposition E, a measure designed to cut cable mileage almost by half. The campaign was peppered with political shenanigans. Master wordsmiths phrased the measure so that a "Yes" on E caused track mileage to be reduced, but you couldn't tell it by the campaign slogan which read, "Keep the cable cars rolling . . . bring back the Hyde Street grip! Vote Yes on E." The measure passed by a narrow margin, and even a successful lawsuit against city officials for unfair tactics didn't stop the track from being torn up. Within two years track mileage had been reduced to the system as we know it today. From its high of 103 miles in 1894, the double track mileage had been reduced to 9.

Still, the efforts of Friedel Klussman and her volunteers are seen as successful, for without their untiring efforts San Francisco would be devoid of cable cars today. In 1971, a ballot measure passed and was written into the City Charter guaranteeing the level of service and perpetuation of lines as they now exist. No alteration or reduction of the current system can be made without the majority approval of city voters — an unlikely event at best.

Friedel Klussmann easily earned her title as "the best friend a cable car ever had".

THE TABLES TURN

Somewhere in the seven year outpouring of love and support from all corners of the earth, it dawned on city officials that in cable cars they had a tourist attraction, a potential revenue producer, a treasure. In the next decade, as a result, the attitude of the city government began to shift. Cable cars graduated to an object of affection. "Without cable cars," columnist Herb Caen immortalized, "San Francisco would be only a lumpy Los Angeles."

Now suddenly city officials were going to bat for the little cars. So impressed was Public Utilities Commissioner James K. Carr that he staged a campaign to attract the attention of the National Park Service in Washington, D.C. The Park Service subsequently designated cable cars a National Landmark — the only rolling one — in November, 1964.

One hundred years after the cable car was born, San Francisco threw it a party to remember. First came the present: Car #1, built from the ground up. Because the craft of building cable cars had been lost, new plans had to be drawn. This was accomplished by comparing old photographs, measuring old cars, then combining the information into working drawings. Car #1 served as focal point for the jubilant celebration at Victorian Square in October, 1973. Cable cars were honored by being named a National Civil Engineering Landmark, and, at the carbarn, the Pacific Coast

The Carpenter shop where cable cars are rebuilt.

Chapter of the Railway and Locomotive Historical Society opened a museum where visitors could learn more about the workings of the oldest — and only — remaining cable car system in the world.

Hardly had the confetti settled from this gala event when it became apparent cable cars faced an entirely new challenge. Age and the burden of 11 million passengers a year were pushing the system to the end of its life cycle. The signs were everywhere. Tracks were so thin they could be chipped by a fingernail. Derailments, from cars running on sagging trackways, were becoming a daily occurence. Every year accidents were increasing in frequency and somberness. For seven years straight the Hyde Street car was involved in runaway accidents. The last, in 1967, claimed two lives.

Recurring depression beam accidents forewarned that mechanical aspects of the system were breaking down. If the beam failed to move aside as the grip hit it, the car would stop dead as if colliding with a wall.

After four such accidents, with multiple injuries to passengers and crew, gripmen and conductors closed the system down in protest. And, in 1976, due to a maintenance backlog, only ten cars were able to go on line.

The Municipal Railway was doing its best to replace and repair, but deterioration was happening faster than corrections could be made. Finally, in 1979, an engineering firm, Chin & Hensolt, was hired to evaluate the damage and to recommend proper procedures to correct it.

The news was not good. Cable car tracks, the report said, were in "acute disrepair", 120 of 635 pulleys were no longer rotating, while the cable had worn deep grooves in others. In October, 1979, the system was shut down for six months, and $1 million was spent on emergency repairs. But these were temporary measures only. If the system was to survive, total restoration was required. The cost — an estimated $58.2 million.

By the late Sixties sagging trackways were causing daily derailments. Accident statistics only became more grim.

RESTORATION

That same determined spirit which saved the cable cars before rallied once again. The press took an invincible stand. LOS ANGELES TIMES' columnist John Dreyfuss wrote, "Besides providing a link with history, the cable cars are fun. Besides being fun they are useful. There is not a lot of useful, historical fun left in American cities. What there is should be saved, and what is saved should be jealously guarded."

On the strength of these and similar sentiments, San Franciscans raised $10 million, the State committed $3.6 million, while the U.S. Department of Transportation, which dubbed cable cars "efficient people movers", contributed the remaining 80 percent, or $44.6 million.

It was almost like starting over. For the trackway to meet the demands of urban traffic, all 69 blocks had to be torn up and replaced. Fourteen foot wide trenches were filled with two concrete trackways reinforced by a network of U-shaped rebar. It was slow work; a given block took ten to twelve weeks to complete. All 40 cars were outfitted with new wheels, axles and slot brakes, and each underwent thorough cosmetic face lifts. Despite determined efforts to standardize, each car managed somehow to retain its own distinct personality.

It took 18 solid months to bring the carbarn up to date. First the demolition squad struck. Everything from cable tunnels to winding machinery was removed. The only things left standing were exterior brick walls and the original smokestack. Then reconstruction began. A new foundation with more than 200 40-foot deep caissons was drilled and poured. To comply with earthquake resistant standards, brick walls were braced by a steel frame and reinforced by concrete. Four 510HP motors were installed to replace the two 700HP motors which had powered the system before. Now each cable had its own independent drive system. An underground viewing room was added so visitors could observe the huge sheaves as they guided cables to and from the barn.

It was a system designed for safety. Where there had been 13 strand alarms before, now there were 60. Depression beams were retooled. Pulleys and sheaves were replaced. Where safety latches had been only at the top of the Hyde Street hill, now they were situated at the crown of every steep hill.

Restoration was slow work. Each of the 69 blocks of trackway took 10 to 12 weeks to tear up and replace.

Restoration of the cable car system took two years and cost more than $58 million.

The conqueror of the hills colorfully, triumphantly, acclaimed.

Cable cars bedecked and ready to celebrate their return to service.

Ambitious though it was, the project was not without problems. Engineers unfortunately forgot they were working with the world's leading authorities on cable cars. Rather than respecting the experts' knowledge, they drew on their own insular experience to redesign different aspects of the system. The swinging arm of the depression beam, for one, was changed from springs to counterweights. Once service was restored, it became an Achilles heel of the system, with crews working one or two nights a week to repair breakdowns. The new turntables did not function well, nor did the holdback or rewinder, the machines used to replace the cable. When millions of dollars are involved, malfunction inevitably raises the question of financial liability, an issue which has been posed by lawyers, but not yet resolved.

Still, the outcome must be viewed as positive. For restoration has added another 100 years to the life of cable cars . . . barring unforeseen earthquakes. If they were a rarity in 1973, consider their historical worth in 2073! And, accidents have been reduced from an average 70 a month pre-restoration to today's 15 a month. Because each cable is now independently driven, when a strand alarm is set off only one cable, as opposed to the entire system, is shut down. As a result, the system is now down half as much as it was before.

Yet, despite its shiny new look, people are still finding ways to improve upon it. For 10 years, up to and throughout restoration, splicer Fred Mueller kept trying to promote a simple device, designed by senior machinist Loy Lew, which would eliminate depression beams. Engineers wouldn't listen. But with the redesigned beams proving to be a nightmare, the alternative finally has been introduced. Lew's device entails removing depression beams and, at the bottom of each hill, simply curving the rail slot around the pulleys. The grip, with the cable in tow, follows the curved slot, and once the car begins its ascent the cable returns to its position beneath the pulleys at the side of the slot. This utterly simple solution just may eliminate the system's most expensive and persistent headache. To which Superintendent of Cable Machinery Don Haagstad replies, "If this works, I think it shows that after 100 years we've learned something."

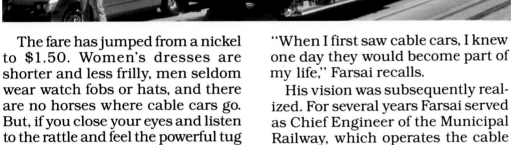

Cable cars bring out the best in those who ride them, and those who work on and with them.

The fare has jumped from a nickel to $1.50. Women's dresses are shorter and less frilly, men seldom wear watch fobs or hats, and there are no horses where cable cars go. But, if you close your eyes and listen to the rattle and feel the powerful tug as the grip grabs hold, the sensation will be the same.

There are few experiences in this stepped-up world that offer as much. Because of this, millions travel from all corners of the earth to ride cable cars, to watch them, to enjoy them. The endearing, enduring little cars bring out the best in them, for when they board, passengers seem to sit or stand happily in awe of a system which would not have been born or survived to today without the gift of human vision and tenacity.

If cable cars bring out the best in those who ride them, they do the same in those who work on and with them. They are a family, a large dedicated talented group of people who mostly love what they do because what they do is unique. Cable cars stand today as a tribute to one man's vision, and many people's capability and caring . . . people like Javan Farsai.

On his first trip to America from Iran as a small boy, Javan's father introduced him to the Statue of Liberty and to San Francisco cable cars.

"When I first saw cable cars, I knew one day they would become part of my life," Farsai recalls.

His vision was subsequently realized. For several years Farsai served as Chief Engineer of the Municipal Railway, which operates the cable car system. During restoration he acted as liaison between consulting engineers and the management of the cable car system. His admiration for the cars remains as pure as his reasons for working with them. "In America we have the Statue of Liberty. We also each have a Statue of Responsibility. Cable cars tell us where we have come from in a mechanical world. It is important for all of America to keep such an old thing going. Because of this, cable cars became my Statue of Responsibility."

His words clearly echo the sentiments of hundreds of men and women who have worked on the system. It is this sense of responsibility, of actual devotion to cable cars that, often against all odds, kept them rolling.

As a result, the invitation stands. Come ride a thrill. It takes only 22 minutes from one end to the other, but in that time you have the chance to travel 100 years back — or two miles forward. The experience, the memories and joy you gain from it, ultimately depend on you.

POINTS OF INTEREST

Today the cable car routes pass buildings and entire city blocks of historic or general significance. These deserve both interest and exploration.

ALONG THE POWELL LINES

• POWELL-MARKET TURNTABLE • Nowhere is enthusiasm for cable cars more apparent than at the Powell lines' starting point. Longest waiting lines for riding the cars form at this, the intersection of San Francisco's two busiest streets. Here, in the past, enthusiastic riders participated in the turning of the car. Standing near this famed turntable offers you a clear view of cable cars as they mount and descend precipitous Powell Street.

• CLAY STREET • Two blocks past California Street, in the shadow of Nob Hill's peak, rests San Fran-

cisco's first cable car route. Clay Street climbs to the sky and descends to the bay on a 19 percent slope. Only a man with Andrew Hallidie's supreme confidence would have risked that grade! More than 100 years later cable cars still hold title as Clay Street's most effective conqueror, though electric trolley buses now travel this route.

• CABLE CARBARN & POWERHOUSE • Perhaps the most noteworthy site along the Powell Street lines is the massive red brick structure situated at Washington and Mason Streets. Here, four cable lines figure-eight their way through massive winding wheels, across suspension pulleys to tension carriages and back to their underground troughs which extend 10-1/2 miles. Drowning all but spectator's awe is the roar of four 510HP motors which operate the system. In the Visitor's Gallery overlooking this operation is one of Hallidie's original cable cars. The building is open to the public from 10:00 a.m. to 6:00 p.m.

• VICTORIAN SQUARE • Line 60 reaches its terminus at Bay and Taylor, an area with a charm all its own.

Cable car cresting the Hyde Street hill with Alcatraz in the background.

Two of San Francisco's most beloved landmarks: colorful Victorian homes and the indefatigable little cable car.

Comings and goings at Victorian Square. Acquatic Park and The Cannery in the background.

Here the mood of the gaslight era is captured by gas lamps and a decorative glass gazebo resting at the foot of the turntable. The Square is fringed by manicured gardens falling to the edge of San Francisco Bay, Aquatic Park with its historic Maritime Museum and its flotilla of historic ships, plus two unique shopping complexes — Ghirardelli Square, a rebuilt chocolate factory, and the Cannery. Drop into the Buena Vista Cafe for a cup of their famous Irish Coffee. The originator of this cafe so loved the cable cars and those who worked them that he placed a codicil in his Will to ensure that cable car operators will always be welcomed in his establishment with free cups of his famous coffee.

• FISHERMAN'S WHARF • The Powell-Mason line terminates just four blocks away at the fringe of this famed site. Once the living quarters and departure point for the city's bustling fishing fleet, today the site has been usurped by commercial entrepeneurs serving tourists. Some exploring will bring you to the piers where the remaining fleet still docks. Hungry? Satisfy your appetite with fresh fish cocktail and San Francisco's famous sourdough French bread purchased from sidewalk concessions while you explore. Nearby Pier 39, San Francisco's newest tourist attraction, offers an exciting array of restaurants and shopping pleasures.

• LOMBARD STREET • At the very crest of the Hyde Street line lies Lombard Street, acclaimed the crookedest street in the world. In the short block, between Hyde and Leavenworth Streets, Lombard changes direction a total of 10 times. It is as much fun to watch as it is to drive, for on any given day during summer more than 3000 automobiles wend their hesitant way down the paved curlicue.

Lombard Street wasn't born crooked. Until 1922 it resembled every other precipitous grade in San Francisco. Only it was steeper than most — 27 percent — and, as such, basically was unmaneuverable by car. So, neighbors petitioned, and the city responded by spending $8,000 to convert straight to serpentine.

For 25 years the curlicue street remained virtually unnoticed and unknown. The wine-importer, gourmet food merchant, and frequent member of the Recreation and Park Commission, Peter Bercut, stepped in. Offended by neighbors' halfhearted attempts at landscaping, Bercut began staging botanical experiments of his own. While on a visit to France he became impressed by a hillside planted in pastel hydrangeas. It pleased him, so, at his own expense, he purchased and imported 2000 of the plants from France to San Francisco. These same 2000 plants, or cuttings from them, paint the street in pastel from spring to fall. A postcard showing the resplendent result, published by H.S. Crocker, sold 278,000 copies in one year!

Lombard Street is as stimulating to walk as it is to drive, so if the mood moves you, hop off the Hyde Street car and walk a crooked block.

ALONG THE CALIFORNIA LINE
Heading West . . .

• MONTGOMERY STREET •
More than a century ago, San Francisco's shoreline stood where Montgomery Street stands today. When San Francisco business needed more room, bay fill began. Buildings sprouted like weeds on this new fill. Within years the tracks of the California line were extended to serve this area. Today Montgomery Street stands as the proud heart of San Francisco's business and financial district.

• BANK OF AMERICA WORLD HEADQUARTERS • This 52-story structure, one of the tallest skyscraper west of Chicago, is impressive not only in height, but also appearance and construction techniques. The building is supported by 50,000,000 pounds of steel . . . enough to produce 12,500 automobiles. The glistening black granite sculpture on its plaza is euphemistically referred to as "the banker's heart".

• OLD SAINT MARY'S • California's pride and San Francisco's Catholic heart is this, the State's first cathedral. Constructed from brick, granite shipped from China and timber from California's own redwood forests, the church, situated at Grant and California, was completed and dedicated in 1854. (For years the Archbishop was criticized for selecting a site so far out of town.) The 1906 earthquake and fire gutted the historic cathedral, leaving only the brick, granite and timber shell. Subsequent years saw careful reconstruction, with both architecture and design duplicating the original where possible. Tended by the Paulist Fathers since 1894, the oldest and most active San Francisco Catholic parish is today a State Landmark.

"Transcendence" by Masayuki Nagare, 1969. This 200-ton black granite sculpture is located at the Bank of America World Headquarters.

Grant Avenue is the main artery of San Francisco's Chinatown, home of the largest population of Chinese people and businesses this side of China.

The bronze fence, which surrounds Pacific Union Club, was a gift from James Flood to his wife in the 1880's.

• GRANT AVENUE • San Francisco's only street with a song written on its behalf ("Grant Avenue, San Francisco" appearing in the musical "Flower Drum Song"), this thoroughfare once comprised the highway to the Barbary Coast, the West's hive of most dangerous criminals. The 1906 fire took its toll, obliterating the sleazy establishments which lined the street. Today Grant Avenue is the main artery of famed Chinatown, the largest population of Chinese people and businesses this side of China.

• NOB HILL • A climb to the stars is also a climb to San Francisco's most historic residential neighborhood, now her most exclusive hotel and apartment district. To take advantage of the spectacular marine view, railroad magnates Leland Stanford, Mark Hopkins, Charles Crocker and Collis P. Huntington, otherwise known as "The Big Four", built their resplendent mansions on top of this hill. When living in San Francisco, Robert Louis Stevenson named it "the hill of palaces".

• STANFORD COURT • Inhabiting the southwest corner of California and Powell, this hotel rests on the site of Leland Stanford's former mansion. Its next door neighbor, the famed Mark Hopkins Hotel, stands on property which served as home to its famous namesake.

• PACIFIC UNION CLUB • All but one mansion was destroyed in the 1906 melee. James C. Flood selected and built his home at the northeast corner of California and Taylor, completing the sandstone structure in 1885. A gift to his wife, Flood then erected a $60,000 bronze fence patterned from a piece of lace Mrs. Flood had seen in a shop window. The fence, which still stands today, was created in Paris, and required a full-time employee to keep it polished. The 1906 Fire gutted the elaborate mansion, but the walls remained. In 1907, the Pacific Union Club, fifth oldest social club in the nation, bought and rebuilt it. Off limits to all but aspiring or actual millionaires, since its dedication in 1911, the Club has permitted women on the premises only twice; once before it opened officially, and again in 1953 when the Club celebrated its 100th Anniversary.

• GRACE CATHEDRAL • Charles Crocker was noted not only for railroad and banking success (Crocker National Bank), but also for philanthropy. When the 1906 tragedy destroyed both his and his son, William's, family mansions on the California block between Taylor and Jones, he donated the property to the Episcopal Diocese of California. Then began, in 1910, the construction of Grace Cathedral. Depression, wars and lack of funds braked construction repeatedly, stalling completion and formal dedication 54 years (1964). Visible from cable cars are the golden Ghiberti Doors, exact replicas of the famed "Gates of Paradise" in Florence, Italy.

• POLK STREET • Natives call it "Polk Gulch", since land configuration deems this the lowest point between Nob Hill and Pacific Heights. In 1906, two days after the earthquake, the block between Polk and Van Ness was intentionally blown up to halt the fire from des-

troying the neighborhoods west of Van Ness.

• VAN NESS AVENUE • One of San Francisco's busiest thoroughfares, Van Ness Avenue brings us to the end of the California line.

The Golden Gate Bridge, gateway to the City by the Bay, home of the world's only remaining cable cars.